# Spurs Were a-Jinglin'

# SPURS WERE a-JINGLIN'
## A brief look at the Wyoming range country

by Don Hedgpeth / photographs by Charles J. Belden

Northland Press

*To Sug*

# Contents

# Introduction

THE PICTURES IN THIS BOOK represent only a small portion of the remarkable photographic record of the Wyoming range left by Charles J. Belden. He was born in San Francisco, California, on November 26, 1887; graduated from Massachusetts Institute of Technology in 1910; and operated the Pitchfork Ranch, west of Meeteetse, Wyoming, from 1914 until the early 1940s.

The Pitchfork, where Belden took these photographs, was founded by Count Otto Franc von Liechtenstein, a German nobleman. Otto Franc, as he was known in the West, came to Wyoming in 1879. He settled on the headwaters of the Greybull River in the Big Horn Basin country just to the east of Yellowstone Park. Franc registered the ⊔⌐ brand and brought the first cattle into the Big Horn Basin.

In 1903 Franc was killed in what was apparently a hunting accident, and the Pitchfork ownership passed to Louis G. Phelps, a Montana banker and cattleman. Phelps proceeded to acquire title to strategic water and grasslands adjoining Franc's original holdings. Sheep were introduced on the Pitchfork during this time.

In 1922 management of the Pitchfork operation passed to Phelps' son and son-in-law, Eugene Phelps and Charles J. Belden. The Pitchfork is still a working ranch today although the land has been portioned off among several of the Phelps' heirs.

The cattle and horses are better bred today and the cowboys dress a little differently, but the spirit of the Wyoming cow country is still much in evidence on the Pitchfork.

With his camera, and with the eye of a knowledgeable cowman, Belden was able to capture images of the rawhide kind of cowboy life before it had undergone the drastic changes of the modern age. The men in Belden's pictures were the kind who could talk with a cow in her own language, and they were always ill at ease on foot. Belden was sympathetic to their way of life. His compassion and understanding for his subject made him something more than just a fine photographer. Charles Belden was an artist. Using a camera instead of paint and brush, he did for his time what Charlie Russell had done for the cow country a generation before.

The Belden pictures are not just photographs in the sense of those produced by L. A. Huffman, of Montana. Belden is closer in comparison to the great Texas range photographer Erwin E. Smith.

The pictures in this book constitute something more than a candid, on the scene, record of Pitchfork ranch life. They show an artist's attention to composition, perspective, and light values, as well as that most necessary ingredient in all fine art, a sense of the spirit of the subject matter.

A collection of more than two thousand negatives are an important part of the archives collection at the Buffalo Bill Historical Center in Cody, Wyoming. Here, the photographic legacy of Belden has a good home, "just down the road a piece" from the Pitchfork range.

Charles Belden died in Florida on February 1, 1966. He was a Wyoming cowman and his photographs are a rich contribution to the history of the range cattle industry.

# Wyoming: Cow Country

WYOMING IS A WORD and a place that evokes images of cowboys, cowhorses, and cattle. The history of no other state is more strongly tied to cattle industry origins than is Wyoming.

Before the cow, Wyoming was but a stretch of the wagon trail on the pioneer route to Utah, California, or the fertile valleys of Oregon Territory. It was home for a handful of army posts; for proud Indian tribes, such as the Sioux and Cheyenne; and for large herds of deer, antelope, and buffalo. Wyoming's rich resources of abundant grass and water remained untapped. The ranges were big, empty, and peaceful; hundreds of miles of nothing but free grass, rushing water, lofty mountains and clean, clear air. There were over a hundred varieties of native grass. Lush bluestem, gramma, and buffalo grass cured on the ground in the dry climate and provided nutritious feed year round.

Rivers with names like Chugwater, Tongue, Belle Fourche, Platte, Wind, Powder, and countless creeks and streams provided a generous supply of fresh water for cow operations in every region of the state. Snowmelt gave a head start for spring grass growth each year. It was an ideal cow country, bountifully endowed with all the necessities for producing beef.

The western range cattle industry made its first dramatic stirrings in the brush country of Southern Texas at the close of the Civil War. The trail driving era began in earnest in 1866, when one-half million longhorns were trailed north from Texas to the shipping pens of the wild Kansas cowtowns. This mass exodus of Texas cattle reached Wyoming that same year, as Nelson Story trailed a beef herd through hostile Indian country on his way to the gold fields of Montana.

The following year the Union Pacific Railroad, building slowly westward across the Great Plains, reached Cheyenne. With a shipping artery to the eastern markets, and more than fifty million acres of unfenced grasslands, Wyoming was destined to be cow country.

John Iliff, the prominent Colorado cowman, trailed the first cattle into the newly-built shipping pens at Cheyenne in 1867. One of the state's first permanent beef herds was established by W. G. Bullock and B. B. Mills on the Laramie Plains in 1868. Others followed quickly, and in a short time what had been buffalo range for centuries became home for vast herds of beef cattle.

Fierce bands of Indian warriors were a major threat to the growth of cattle operations in the 1870s. But the endless tide of cattle sweeping up from Texas, the vast ranges of free grass, the railroad, and the favorable eastern market for beef all provided powerful incentive to horseback men with guts and good credit.

By the mid-1880s, the open range cattle industry was at its zenith. Rapid expansion, heavy foreign investment and sheer magnitude of operation in Wyoming's cow country reflected all of the most glorious aspects of the rawhide era of the double-tough cowpuncher. The land was free, taxes were low and credit was plentiful.

Nature dealt a killing blow to the Wyoming ranges in the winter of 1886–1887. Cow outfits suffered staggering death losses in the continuous blizzards that had followed a drouthy summer and fall. Additionally, the eastern market for beef had become glutted, and cattle prices fell drastically.

But the genuine cowmen were of a tough fiber. They would not stay whipped. As they rebuilt their operations they scaled down their herd numbers with an eye to supply and demand, introduced pure-blooded bulls to increase the quality of their beef, and began to put up hay as insurance against another severe winter. They also began to gain title to their ranges as a protection from the ever-increasing numbers of sheepmen and homesteaders who were looking for a share of the grassland.

The organization of the Wyoming Stock Growers' Association in 1879 provided a power base for the cattle interest. Up into the early 1900s, the W.S.G.A. exerted an influence in the state equal, if not superior, to that of the legislature. Their membership was well represented in the legislature, the governor's office, and in Congress. They were men dedicated to their chosen life. One old-timer reflected: "We loved those cattle and those horses and the life with them. We didn't have anything else to love, I guess."

The most dramatic and controversial episode of the western range cattle industry occurred on the eastern slope of Wyoming's Big Horn Mountains in 1892. The episode is referred to as the Johnson County War, and it signaled the closing of the era of free grass and gigantic cattle operations.

Following the disastrous winter of 1886–1887, when Wyoming herds were decimated, ranchers were forced to lay off many of their cowboys. These hired men on horseback were not able to find work, and many of them began "appropriating" mavericks and branding calves in advance of the official roundups authorized by the Stock Growers' Association.

The small ranchers who were flooding into Wyoming in ever-increasing numbers sided with the rustlers against the big ranchers. The coalition of rustlers and small land owners constituted a majority in several eastern Wyoming counties. This allowed them to elect their own sheriffs and exert considerable influence on the local courts. Faced with mounting losses to the rustlers, the crunch of a failing cattle market, and no legal recourse, the cowmen took matters into their own hands.

In the spring of 1892, representatives of the big cow outfits and a band of hired Texas gunmen debarked from a special train at Casper and rode north for Buffalo, the county seat of Johnson County.

The group was armed to the teeth, and their mission was the extermination of the rustler element that had been preying on their herds. The expedition, which in the beginning had all the earmarks of a noble and just crusade, turned into a dismal failure. After killing two suspected rustlers during a day-long siege, the "invaders" were themselves besieged by the rustler-settler faction. The Army arrived and put the cowmen and their hired guns under arrest. They were subsequently released, but the significance of their failure to wipe out the rustlers had implications that reached far beyond Johnson County, Wyoming.

It was the last hurrah for the big cowmen. They were no longer beyond the fringe of civilization and a law unto themselves. As one old cowman lamented: "Well, I have my ranch here yet, but I had to get deeds to the land I occupy, as Uncle Sam and I could not agree. We came very near running together once. I thought I was the fellow who discovered that country but he sent a bunch out from Washington and surveyed me out of house and home and told me what I could do. I wanted to treat with them but they would give me no red wagons so I had to take my medicine."

Early Wyoming developed and prospered in direct proportion to the growth and success of her cattle industry. The pioneer cattlemen made Wyoming something of which the West will always be proud.

*Following the spring branding the cattle are trailed to the high ranges and turned loose to spend the summer on the lush grass which is nurtured by the melting of deep snows of the previous winter. The cowboys pause at the end of a drive and have time to enjoy the spectacular country.*

*Cowboys riding in the high country packed in all their food, clothes and their beds for a summer's work. In this picture the two men have paused to look over their charges as they head into a remote line shack where they will make their home until it's time for the fall roundup.*

*A top hand on a Wyoming cow outfit enjoyed the life he had chosen. When the weather was nice, and in between the spring and fall roundups, it was a quiet time, a time to relax in the saddle, look at the new calves and reflect on the wonders of nature.*

8

*The high country provided good grass and water for the cattle in the summer. Periodically, cowboys made their rounds to see if the cattle were faring well. Here a cowboy pauses for an icy drink from a stock pond fed by the snowmelt above timberline.*

*One of the greatest assets of Wyoming's cow country is its abundant water. A cowboy pauses in his day's ride, lets his horse get a long drink and considers how the papa bull is getting along with his girlfriends.*

Here is springtime cow work. Following the roundup, the new calves are roped, drug to the fire and branded with the outfit's coat of arms. The mother cows look on apprehensively as their babies bawl for relief.

A Wyoming cowboy in wintertime was of necessity a tough man. Wallowing through deep snowdrifts, facing cold winds that blew right off the North Pole, and nursemaiding calves who were born too early in the season gave the work a bitter edge not known on the southern ranges.

14

*Summer has always seemed the shortest season of the year in Wyoming. It is warm one day in September, and the next morning there are several inches of snow on the range. The cowboys dressed in all the clothes they had and went on about their work. Heavy coats, wool long-handles, heavy chaps and even big fur mitts helped create an illusion of warmth.*

This is Wyoming cow country in the winter. An early blizzard has made it necessary to bring the cattle down from the mountain ranges to the feeding grounds below. Wyoming is a land of few contrasts in the winter . . . it is all white and all cold. This is one of Belden's classic photographs and was well known to cow people a generation ago when it hung in ranch headquarters and commission company offices throughout the High Plains country.

17

Wyoming can be as cold and bleak as any Eskimo could survive. It is as bitter for the men as it is for the horses and cattle. But there is always springtime ahead. Its promise of green grass and blue sky makes winter almost tolerable.

The snow has begun to melt and the cattle are shaped up for the drive to the high ranges. Cowboys know it means the end of a dreary winter of feeding hay when the snow prevented the cattle from grazing.

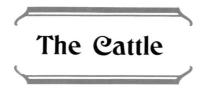

# The Cattle

A CLOSE LOOK at world history will lend much support to the claim that the cow has always been the advance agent of civilization. This was certainly the case in Wyoming.

The first cattle in the state were the oxen which pulled the pioneers' wagons over the Oregon Trail. Following close behind were the teams of the freight companies. The great potential of Wyoming's grasslands was recognized in the 1850s when sore-footed work oxen were wintered on the Laramie Plains. Not only did the weakened cattle survive the harsh winter, they were in excellent condition when spring came.

There were far-sighted cowmen who recognized the treasure in Wyoming grass. Texas longhorns were the first beef herds in the state. In the late 1860s and early 1870s, only steer herds were brought up the trail. They would spend a season on the northern range and were then rounded up and shipped on the railroad to Chicago and other points east. Not only could the southern cattle survive an average northern winter, they also put on more weight and developed faster than they would in Texas. In 1871, a four-year-old grass-fed steer, raised from a calf on the Laramie Plains, yielded 982 pounds of meat, with two inches of fat on his ribs.

The next step in the development of the Wyoming range business was the introduction of stock cattle for breeding. This would supply native herds for the ever-increasing numbers of ranches that were being established, and would provide a desirable alternative to trailing cattle from Texas each spring.

The old longhorn cow played a vital role in the founding of native Wyoming herds. She had "weather wisdom," and was a great provider and protector for her calves with her native instincts for finding water and grass. By 1876, Oregon stockers were being trailed eastward into Wyoming. These northwest "shorthorns," when cross-bred with the Texas cattle, did much to upgrade the quality of the beef.

In 1870 there were about eleven thousand cattle on Wyoming grass; by 1886 the number had risen to an estimated total of almost nine hundred thousand. Wyoming had become something more than just a winter pasture and a cow trail. The territory was prospering and growing right along with, and because of, the cattle business. One old cowpuncher recalled those days: "There was no other industry in the territory, so there was nothing else to talk about but cow and bull (the cow's husband, and a good deal of the other kind)."

Alexander Swan, who at one time operated six hundred thousand acres and ran over one hundred thousand head of cattle, was the first man to introduce purebred Hereford bulls to the Wyoming range. When bred to a Hereford bull, the old longhorn cow produced calves that retained much of the momma's "hustling" ability, as well as the improved beef qualities of the papa.

Through the years the longhorn characteristics have been bred out of Wyoming cattle. But oldtime cowmen are mindful of the significant role played by that hardy strain.

The introduction of Hereford cattle assured the upbreeding of the southern longhorns and the Oregon crosses. It laid the foundations of a quality reputation for Wyoming grass-fed, white-faced cattle that has endured down to the present day. Most all the popular beef breeds of cattle are represented on Wyoming's ranches today, but the pillars were the longhorn and the Hereford.

22

With improved bloodlines for better beef animals, and a host of management innovations, the Wyoming cow was one of the proudest standard-bearers in the pageant of the open range. The northeastern United States may owe a lot to the *Mayflower* and the Pilgrims; Wyoming owes as much to the cow.

*In the spring, the bulls run with the cows in the high mountain meadows. Here a range country monarch bellows his virility and for a moment sheds ages of domestication and becomes a wild animal in a wide, wild country.*

*A healthy, alert calf considers Wyoming springtime and wonders what the world is all about. His education will begin shortly when he's gathered with his mother in the roundup and suffers the indignity of castration and branding.*

24

Cattle are born but reluctant swimmers. Here the cattle convey themselves across the Shoshone River on the way to the shipping pens at Cody.

At the spring roundup, a new calf learns about cowboys as his time comes at the branding fire. The calf's mother looks on with concern, and perhaps remembers her first spring.

Brands are the mark of ownership of a particular cow outfit. They constitute a heraldry of the range. A cowman's pride in his brand is as strong as any nobleman's was for his coat of arms in the days of knighthood.

29

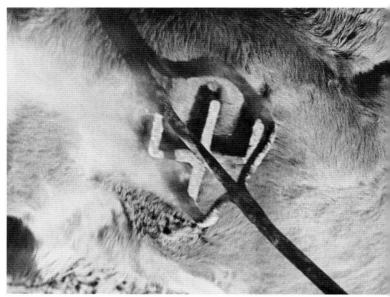

*The Pitchfork brand is the mark of the Wyoming ranch where Charles Belden, cowman and photographer, took the remarkable photographs included in this book. It is a historic brand in Wyoming and is still in use today, marking a proud cow country heritage.*

*As the cowboys ride among the cattle on the summer pastures, they often find calves that were dropped after the spring roundup. Here, the men are using a cinch-ring to brand a calf that was born too late for the formalities of the roundup. In early Wyoming, the cinch-ring was a favorite branding tool of the rustlers.*

*Working chutes such as these changed the nature of a lot of cattle work. It enabled the hands to work more efficiently than when they roped and branded out in the open, but it wasn't as appealing to the real hands who prided themselves on the job they could do horseback.*

31

*There is little relief for cattle caught out in the open during a Wyoming blizzard. Hump up, turn tail to the wind and take it is the only option.*

*This tragedy on the range is repeated many times each year when late snowstorms hit the herds during calving time. This little dogie can't find his mama, and his only salvation — a cowboy.*

*Wyoming cows have to be good mothers. In country like this, strong mothering instincts can be as important a breeding consideration as good beef quality.*

Cowboys and cows can partner up at times and help each other. Usually it's one-sided with the cowboys providing all the help. Here man helps a mama get her new baby out of the early spring snow and back to the protection of the feeding ground.

It is the nature of horses bred and raised in ranch country to hump up and buck from time to time. Here, at an early day Pitchfork rodeo, the broncs were saddled and rode out in the open, with the spectators forming the arena. You didn't have to look further than the ranch to find snaky horses for this kind of action.

# The Horses

IT WAS A FACT OF LIFE in the open range days that "a man afoot was no man at all." The ranch horse, or cow pony, has always been man's partner in the business of raising beef. Good horses in early Wyoming were as necessary to the cattle business as grass and water.

Ranch horses came to Wyoming with the men and cattle from Texas. Most of the horses in any cow outfit's remuda were about half bronc; the kind that could throw a man so high "he could land on his feet running and not fall down," or "kick a chew of tobacco out of your mouth, and do everything mean."

There are legends connected with outlaw cow ponies in the early Wyoming range country that match those of the bronc peelers that rode them. The modern sport of rodeo had its origins in the roundup camps where men tested their skill and risked their necks and their pride to ride a horse with a bad reputation.

The little Spanish cow ponies from Texas thrived on the lush grass of Wyoming. The infusion of several strains of eastern draft horse breeds developed a bigger horse for the Wyoming remudas than the native Texas mounts. Most of the original cow outfits were not in the horse breeding business and used only geldings in the cow work. But as the cattle business boomed in the 1880s, horse ranching became a business in its own right. Wyoming still produces fine ranch horses, with a big frame Quarter Horse being the predominant breed.

Many of the early cowpunchers liked to brag about their top horse: "He's a real cow horse, gentle as a child, and kind as a cooing dove; quick as a cat and surefooted as a mountain goat, and has brains enough to savvy Mexican and count money."

On the open range each working cowhand was assigned a string of ranch-owned horses. The number of mounts in a man's string depended on such things as the prosperity of the outfit, how rough the country was, and the kind of work to be done at a particular time of year. An average Wyoming cowpuncher's string was six to eight head of geldings.

Included in a cowboy's string were horses with specialized talents. A cowboy had his particular favorites for the big morning sweeps of the spring and fall roundups; cutting horses for herd work during the seasons of the spring branding and the fall shipping; and a night horse for standing watch with the herd during roundup or on the trail. Some boys liked to brag on a good swimmer which was a real blessing when crossing the swollen rivers of Wyoming springtime.

The cowboy's feelings about his horse, good or bad, were quite different than his attitude toward the cattle. Even though he might not own a horse of his own and rode only ranch geldings, he felt for his horse in a way that he never felt for the cattle. As distorted as the relationship has been by the Zane Grey kind of writers and the Hollywood B westerns, the cowboy and horse were partners in the kind of work they did.

Many men were sentimental about the horses they rode and remembered them fondly in later years. To others, the horse was just a means of transportation in going about the business of cowboying. But whatever their feelings were about the horses they rode, all good hands looked after their mounts closely. Horses in working shape were a vital necessity in any ranching enterprise. An old range axiom says: "A cow outfit is only as good as its horses."

*In the early morning a cowboy wrangles the mounts for the day's work.*

*Good horses have always been as important to big cattle operations as grass and water. Wyoming horses are bigger in frame and foot than their cousins in the southwest cattle country. They are much better able to look after themselves in a hard winter than cattle.*

*Pack horses have been as important as cowhorses on the big Wyoming outfits. These are being loaded with salt for the cattle grazing up on the mountains during the summer. Packing was a special skill that southern cowboys did not necessarily learn, but it was a must for the Wyoming cowhands.*

*It was the horse and not the cow that made cowboys. It is the horse that sets cowboys apart from the herdsmen who work on foot. This proud horseman is distributing salt for the cattle in the high ranges. His good horses are a continuing source of pride.*

*A cowboy brings down a bunch of horses from the high country, or moves them to better grazing. His bed is tied on to one of the loose horses, indicating he will be away from the bunkhouse for awhile.*

*As the time approaches for roundup, the horse herds are brought in to the ranch headquarters. They are shod, fed a little corn and rode a bit to take out any of the kinks that might have developed in their backs.*

A top hand's reputation had a lot to do with the kind of horses in his string. A good roper and a good roping horse got to do the top job of moving in the herd, roping and dragging out the calves. Other hands, not as well mounted, had to work on the ground, wrestling with the calves and running back and forth to the branding fire.

Range-bred colts were never eager to pack men around on their backs. Horse breaking was a vital activity associated with any big cow outfit. In this photograph, a big bronc has been fore-footed in the corral and sets the mood for the fireworks to come when the first cowboy steps aboard him.

46

*A good hand respected and appreciated his good horses. Their welfare was always intertwined, for "a man afoot was no man at all."*

*A man who made his living as a cowpuncher often became more comfortable around his horses than he was with people off the ranch. Bragging about the horses in your string was always a topic of conversation when cowboys got together.*

A cowboy heads for work on the summer ranges. He is self-sufficient. The pack horses carry all the food and housekeeping tools he'll need until he gets back to the ranch in the fall, or until someone packs him in new provisions. He even has his two dogs for company.

*Faithful cow horses wait patiently outside a line shack as snow piles up in the saddles. The saddles have ropes tied on, and there is bound to be work that needs doing, yet the cowboys stay for just one more cup of hot coffee.*

*A good fiddle player was, in his own right, as respected as a top cowboy in the early days on the Wyoming range. His hoe-downs and ballads added seasoning to the bland monotony of life in the cow camp. The old fiddle player shows the mark of many years spent in the open. But he smiles at the pleasure he is able to bring others and is grateful that he can still be around the only kind of men he ever knew.*

# The Men

THE COWBOY WAS OF A BREED that was bound to be wild and brave. Wyoming presented perhaps the broadest range of the types of men who became cowboys. A considerable number of the early Wyoming hands were Texans. They had followed the longhorns north to a land that looked like it would be cow country forever. Some were fiercely un-reconstructed rebels; some Mexican vaqueros. The Texas men were the genuine article, though, regardless of their individual backgrounds.

A great many Wyoming cowboys were easterners. Cities like Boston were represented in significant numbers. These easterners were usually of fine families; hardy young men who craved a kind of adventure that could not be found in their home states. An early Powder River cow-man noted that: "It took four years for a Boston feller to go through Harvard College to fit him to come to Wyoming to learn cowpunching at thirty dollars per month." To the east, in the Dakota country, Teddy Roosevelt was one of the best known of the easterners who aspired to earn their spurs.

Remittance men from the titled families of several countries were also in evidence on the early Wyoming ranges.

The conflict of cultures was dramatic. A fall roundup quite often found a young English blue blood, a Harvard man, and a Texas boy who could neither read nor write, starting out together on the morning circle. The Southwesterners generally remained thirty-dollar-a-month hands. The better-heeled Europeans and easterners most often sought the distinction of cowman by buying into a ranching operation. As was said in that day, "Cow punching, as seen from the veranda of the Cheyenne Club, was a most attractive proposition."

In spite of their differing origins and motivations, the work was an equalizer in the rugged life of the cow camp. Those who made a hand were all men of whang-leather toughness. Some of them were like the horses they rode — "they would not do to monkey with." The harshness of their life was reflected in their creased, tanned faces; and in the bow of their legs, and the stoop of their shoulders.

Cowboys became as natural a part of Wyoming as the antelope and deer. A cowboy lived in harmony, when he could, with nature. It was a life close to the ground. The men who chose it were "bound to be wild and brave. They put their faith in God, a six-shooter and the chuck-wagon, and went about the business of cowboying."

The cowmen viewed their hands from different perspectives. Two of the most prominent of all those who had large stakes in the cattle business were John Clay of Wyoming, and Charles Goodnight of Texas.

Colonel Goodnight said of his men: "I wish I could find words to express the trueness, the bravery, the hardihood, the sense of honor, the loyalty to their trust and to each other. . . ."

Mr. Clay expressed a different opinion: "The chief obstacle of the range was the cowboys, who were mostly illiterate, uncivilized; who drank and thieved and misbranded cattle, and with a kind of rough loyalty, never told on one another in their crimes."

The truth about cowboys, then and now, lies somewhere in between those two assessments. The great painter of range life, Charlie Russell, said of cowboys: "If they are human, they're a separate species."

*This young man's face shows something of the pride he felt about "earning his spurs" and making a hand. He sits on his horse straight up and would throw a rope on anything that crossed his path just for the fun of it. He wouldn't have traded places with anyone you could have named.*

*Men who worked for a particular outfit shared a pride in their outfit that rivaled and often surpassed that of the outfit's owner. They also shared with each other a feeling of accomplishment in doing a man's work. Most of all, they shared a sense of loneliness that grew with each year they spent away from homes and families.*

*The romance of the Zane Grey cowboy is not evident in this great photograph of a genuine range man. There could be no more graphic representation of winter in Wyoming's cow country than this picture. The horse's breath and body heat is turning to ice and the man's tight-lipped face and his humped shoulders betray his discomfort. You can bet they were double-tough men.*

The isolation of ranch life was the toughest thing to which a young cowboy had to adjust. Memories of family and home were still vivid and the occasional letter from his mother, or a sweetheart, put his desire for cowboying to a hard test. The ties loosened with each passing year and whenever he did visit the folks at home, he was uncomfortable and anxious to get back to the ranch.

*A cowboy, a good ranch horse and country that looks like it did when it was buffalo range. This photograph is timeless in its subject. The grandfather of the man shown could have ridden through this same country, his own grandson may yet pass this way, and very little would distinguish the generations, one from another, in the remote corners of the big ranches.*

*When men like these got together for a smoke and conversation the topics were usually the same. They talked about the work just finished, or yet to be done; about the weather and the condition of the range; about a promising new colt they were riding; and less frequently about their homes and maybe a girl whose picture they still carried.*

60

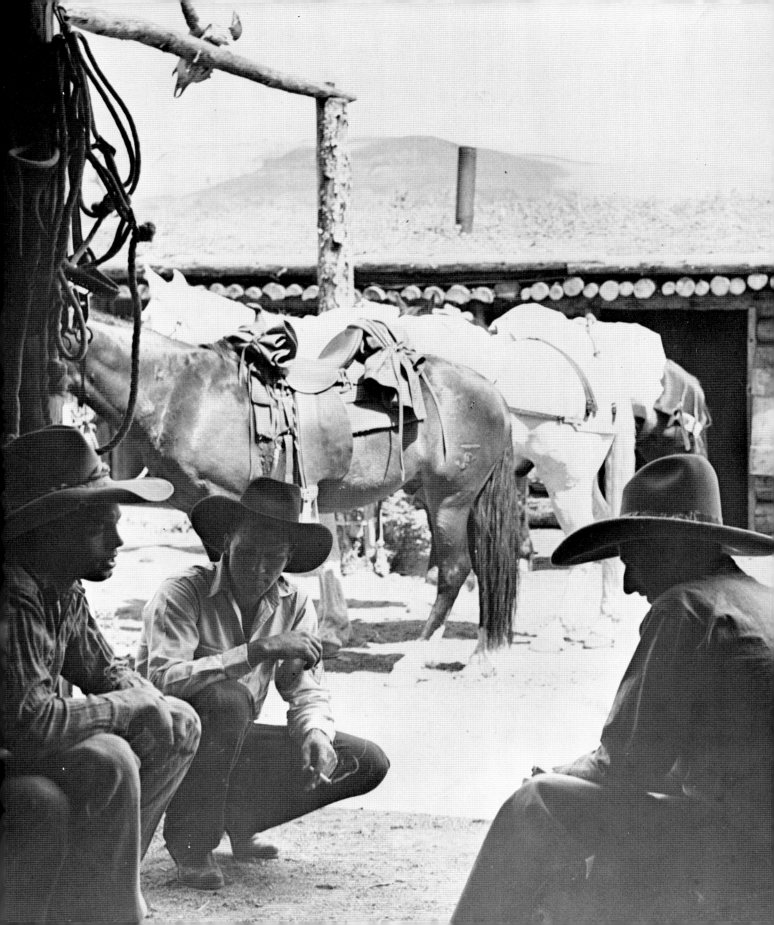

*A range man always dressed from the top down. Accordingly, this cowpuncher is pulling on his boots last and note that the spurs are already strapped on. He had no reason to take the spurs off his boots at the end of a day since he wasn't going anywhere but to bed. In cow camps like this a man had to sleep quick to get any rest at all.*

This is the way life was for a cowboy in a Wyoming line camp. He used a bed he could roll and pack on a horse; rolled his own smokes, carried a pistol for two- and four-legged predators; rubbed his stove-up joints with liniment, slept in his clothes for warmth and on especially cold nights threw his angora chaps on the bed for a little extra warmth; and started his day early.

63

The fall roundup was to gather the beef steers for shipping. Wyoming shipping, until recently, meant long trains of cattle cars bound for such faraway places as Chicago. These boys are wore to a nub after a week's drive from the ranch to the railroad and all the work of loading the cars. But they are embarking on a big adventure as they get a free ride in the caboose to look after the cattle on the long trip. The bright lights at the other end of the ride held promise of adventures to be remembered during the coming winter back at the ranch.

*Old timers like this were affected by the long, lonesome times they spent out by themselves. They made friends with their horses and maybe with a dog, or a cat. This man is feeding his pet from an old coffee can as he ties a honda knot in a new catch rope. This kind of man knew what the cow said to her calf, but he was awkward in the presence of his own kind. He was a cowboy.*

When old cowpunchers were no longer able to hold a riding job they became lost souls. Riding after cattle was all they knew and when they could do that no more their spirits shriveled and died. In this picture the old man tends the branding fire and prepares injections for the cattle, and recalls when he roped the calves and drug them in to the fire. But it was a long time ago.

*One of the genuine characters of the old time cow outfits was the cook. He commanded authority second only to that of the cow boss and was supreme in his own realm, be it the cookhouse at the ranch, or the chuck wagon out on the range. Many times he was an old cowpuncher too stove-up to work horseback. This fact, and the complexities of his work, tended to make him cranky. He was vital to range work, because cowboys, like soldiers, travel on their stomachs.*

*Here is a prototype of the old cowpuncher who came up the trail from Texas and stayed on to be a principal character in the early drama of the Wyoming range. During his life he saw the transition from free grass open ranges, when men could ride from Texas to Alberta without opening a gate, to the days when barbed wire and hay farming forced cowboys to work on foot.*

*Cowboys, alone or in pairs, spent the winter in remote line cabins in the distant corners of the big outfits. They rode out each day to check the condition of the cattle, and to lend a helping hand where needed. It was a seven-day routine and was most necessary when the weather was at its worst.*

70

# The Life

BEING A RANGE COWBOY anywhere was a tough line of work to follow. Winter weather added extra harshness in Wyoming's cow country. Riding the ranch boundaries for drifting cattle and tailing up the weak ones in deep snow and bitter cold called for rugged men.

There seemed always to be men to take on the job; men who never failed to laugh at every hardship and danger. A young Texas cowpuncher wintered on Box Elder Creek north of Cheyenne in the '80s. He remembered the experience: "I did not know until then that I was so tough. I was from Texas but could wallow in snow at thirty degrees below zero." A lot of the southern boys would roll their bed and drift as soon as "the geese began to move."

The long days of spring roundup seemed never to end. It was forking salty horses before daylight, riding circle to gather the cattle by noon each day, cutting the herd, castrating and branding the new calves. Following the spring work the cattle were often driven to the high ranges where the grass was lush from the moisture of the melting snow.

During the summer months, Wyoming cowboys rounded up the stock horses and branded the new colts. The rest of the summer was spent checking the cattle in the high ranges and breaking colts for a new bunch of cow horses.

With fall came the beef roundup. Late calves were branded, and all that year's calves were cut away from their mamas for weaning. The mature steers were selected and cut for shipping. By November the beef steers had been driven to the railroad and shipped east. Early Wyoming outfits generally laid off most of the hands after shipping. This set a lot of boys loose with winter coming on. Some went back home to see their families; others to a remote line camp to look after the cattle or maybe to run a trap line. Life in a line shack during a Wyoming winter made a man feel more alone than any man ever was.

After years of cowboying for scant wages they had nothing but the experience to show for it all, and they generally had paid a high price for that. It was all hard work when there was work to be done. But there was a dignity in doing it horseback. Half-broke horses and snorty mama cows kept it from being boring. They used to like to boast that they could go anywhere a cow would and stand anything a horse could.

There was a large measure of independence to life on the Wyoming range. Self-reliance and vitality were essential qualities of a top hand. The men took pride in their kind of life and in the cow work they did. Loyalty to the brand they rode for was a strong bond between the men of a particular outfit. They would follow their wagon boss "through hell and never complain."

It was a life of early mornings, long days and short nights. Plain, hardy food and plenty of horseback work kept the fat trimmed from their frames. As one cowman put it: "They live on little and are as loyal in their promises and their sympathies as they are ardent in their vengeance."

The Wyoming cowboy had a taste of genuine life, and while it lasted, he savored every bit of it. His motto was: "Take her as she comes and like it."

*A morning's circle has been made and the cattle are held for the afternoon's work. In the spring the calves are worked; in the fall the beef steers are separated for shipping to market.*

*Spring is a time of vitality on the range. New calves are born, the snow melts, green grass grows anew and the cowboy's juices began to pump as the roundup gets under way. It's a new season in ranch country and it feels good to shed heavy clothes and be out doing cow work on a good horse again.*

*The cattle have shorter horns and the men dress a little differently, but the process of moving cattle remains pretty much the same as it was when the herds came up the Texas trails in the 1880s.*

*A cowboy pauses beside a mountain tank to see how the cattle are faring and to look off across the wide vistas of one of God's most perfect cow countries.*

*One of the most dangerous of all the cowboy's chores was swimming a herd across a swollen, springtime river. If the cattle bunched and turned back, a man could be caught in the tangle. If he ever lost his horse, the weight of boots and chaps made swimming in the strong current impossible. As many men were killed crossing herds in rivers as in prairie stampedes during the days before the fencer came.*

Early morning in a roundup camp and there was a chill in the air, be it April or September. In the Wyoming country, a good outfit bragged of a cook tent in addition to the chuck wagon and with a wood stove to boot. The remuda is held by a single rope corral stretched between the trees behind the wagon. The men get ready to mount with a good chance that a few of the horses will be a little snuffy in the crisp morning air.

79

*On the roundup ground, the top hands ride among the cattle and rope out the new calves. This man ropes the head, whereas other outfits preferred to have the calves heeled so they wouldn't choke down while being drug to the branding fire.*

*The cowboys working on the ground were called muggers and flankers. They throw the calves and hold them while the branding and the castration of the bull calves is done. It is a dirty, hot job, and they envy the roper.*

*A worried mother follows her calf out of the herd, and if the cowboys don't do their work in quick order, she may scatter the whole outfit with a vengeance.*

When the cattle could be worked in pens the chores went quicker. Here two good hands have penned a small bunch and are branding, in this case, a pretty good sized calf. The horse shown is any cowboy's pride. With no rider on his back, he keeps the heel rope tight and proves he is a sure-enough cow horse.

*Tough horses make tough men. Range colts were never pets you could bribe with sugar. Older horses that were not broke, or had become spoiled, required stout medicine. If a horse wouldn't pack a cowboy and do a share of the work, he had no place on the ranch. Some men were valued for their special abilities as "bronc stompers." Here such a man is ringing the school bell and class is about to start.*

*The roundup outfit heads out from ranch headquarters. The chuck wagon carries the grub, the cowboys' beds and a good supply of branding irons for the work ahead. The remuda trails along, pausing at every chance to nip at the new spring grass.*

*Day breaks early during roundup. Coffee is already boiling, hung over the fire with a Pitchfork branding iron. As soon as breakfast is done, the boys will roll their beds, catch up their horses and begin the morning sweep to gather cattle in a particular area.*

The chuck wagon was the hub of life during the fall and spring roundups. Here the men slept, ate, rubbed horse liniment on their aches and swapped lies with each other. The Z/T brand on the side of the wagon signifies one of the divisions of the Pitchfork outfit.

*For a few minutes following the noon meal, the cow-boys shoot dice and enjoy the shade of the wagon as they wait for the branding irons to heat. The man standing at the back of the wagon is a visitor in camp and not a hand, as is clearly indicated by his clothes.*

This remarkable photograph is a classic representation of the changes that came to the Wyoming ranges. Here the old roundup wagon with its teams has given way to the machine age. The Pitchfork chuckbox is in evidence, as are the cowboys' beds, and a spare saddle is cinched to the hood. This foretold the coming of the pickup, a necessary and useful tool in today's ranch country.

91

*The origin of the term "cowpuncher" is said to have come from the loading of cattle on train cars for shipment to market. The men who used the prod-poles to "punch" the cattle up the ramp and into the cars were usually not cowboys. Down through the years the terms "cowboy" and "cowpuncher" have become synonymous, although a few old cowboys still resent the latter label.*

*The cattle have been loaded and the cowboys pause to visit with the ranch owner and cattle buyers. After the hard work of shipping, the boys have put on their good shirts and are ready for a night on the town before heading back to the ranch.*

93

*Feed for the cattle is a constant concern when there's
snow on the ground. Unlike horses, cattle won't paw
through to the grass. The cowboy moves a small bunch
to the feeding grounds and haystacks, or possibly to a
little valley meadow up against the mountains where
the snow doesn't drift.*

*Much of the romance of cowboy life was forgotten
when the hard winters blew cold and blizzards swept
the ranges of Wyoming. Another Belden classic.*

*Cowboys are as natural a part of Wyoming as the antelope and elk. They are at home here, just as the Indian once was. It has remained a country with a strong horseback tradition.*

*Changes came to the Wyoming range, but in spite of the encroachments of the machine age, the man and his horse remained the two keys to the success of the cattle industry.*

# Epilogue

THE RANGE CATTLE INDUSTRY in Wyoming seemed to spring up all at once. In the decade of the 1880s it grew from a few scattered steer herds to a gigantic and prosperous industry. Just as quickly it declined, but it came back after that terrible winter of 1886–1887. And this time it came to stay.

The cow country heritage is still strong in Wyoming. Cattle were the foundation upon which Wyoming was built. There is still loyalty to the cow and the industry she produced.

In spite of killing winters, drought, depression, bureaucrats and "conservationists," the cowman has endured. He has steadfastly spurned government subsidies, and, in the face of constantly rising operational costs, has maintained the independence and integrity of his industry.

New calves still hit the ground each spring in Wyoming. Men still pack ropes on their saddles and go about the business of putting beef on the dinner tables of America. The cattle are of a different kind today, and the ranches are smaller, but the nature of the work and the spirit of the men who are involved in it are much the same as they were when drovers first crossed the Platte at Ogallala and headed west into God's most perfect cattle ranges.

# Selected Bibliography

THE FOLLOWING IS A BIBLIOGRAPHIC LISTING that pretty well covers the subject of Wyoming range cattle history. It is not complete, but represents a variety of titles, of varying degrees of significance, from my own collection.

Six of the items are official publications of the Wyoming Stock Growers' Association and are fundamental to any range cattle history library.

I have listed several Johnson County War titles, and there are several others on this same subject that I did not include. This incident on the Wyoming range, much like the Custer Battle, is of a singular nature and continues to attract attention and controversy.

BABER, D. F. and WALKER, BILL. *The Longest Rope*. Caldwell, Idaho: The Caxton Printers, 1940. Another subjective treatment of the Johnson County War.

BRAYER, HERBERT O. *Range Murder: A Vignette of the Johnson County War in Wyoming*. Evanston, Illinois: The Branding Iron Press, 1955.

BURNS, ROBERT HOMER; GILLESPIE, ANDREW SPRINGS; and RICHARDSON, WILLING GAY. *Wyoming's Pioneer Ranches*. Laramie: Top of The World Press, 1955. A source book of the same kind of richness but disorderly structure as *The Trail Drivers of Texas*.

BURROUGHS, JOHN ROLFE. *Guardian of the Grasslands: The First Hundred Years of the Wyoming Stock Growers Association*. Cheyenne: Wyoming Stock Growers' Association, 1971. The most recent and most comprehensive of the histories of the W.S.G.A.

BURT, MAXWELL STRUTHERS. *Powder River; Let 'Er Buck*. New York and Toronto: Farrar and Rinehart, Inc., 1938.

CANTON, FRANK M. *Frontier Trails*. Boston and New York: Houghton Mifflin Co., 1930. The posthumously published autobiography of one of the most dramatic characters of the Old West. Canton was a principal figure in the Johnson County War.

CLAY, JOHN. *My Life on the Range*. Chicago: privately printed, 1924. This key book was privately printed by one of the prime movers of the Wyoming range cattle industry.

DAVID, ROBERT B. *Malcolm Campbell, Sheriff*. Casper, Wyoming: Wyomingana, Inc., 1932. This book also treats the Johnson County War.

FREWEN, MORETON. *Melton Mobray, and Other Memories*. London: Herbert Jenkins, Ltd., 1924. Contains ten chapters of this Englishman's ranching experiences in early Wyoming.

FRINK, MAURICE. *Cow Country Cavalcade*. Denver: Old West Publishing Co., 1954. This is one of the six authorized histories of the Wyoming Stock Growers' Association published at approximately ten year intervals since 1923.

FRINK, MAURICE; JACKSON, W. TURRENTINE; and SPRING, AGNES WRIGHT. *When Grass Was King*. Boulder, Colorado: University of Colorado Press, 1956.

GREENBURG, DON W. *Sixty Years, a Brief Review of the Cattle Industry in Wyoming*. Cheyenne: Wyoming Stock Growers' Association, 1932. This pamphlet was the second historical work published by the Wyoming Stock Growers' Association.

GRESS, KATHRYN. *Ninety Years in Cow Country*. Wyoming Stock Growers' Association, 1963. Another of the W.S.G.A. sponsored histories.

GUERNSEY, CHARLES ARTHUR. *Wyoming Cowboy Days*. New York: G. P. Putnam's Sons, 1936.

HUNT, FRAZIER. *The Long Trail From Texas: The Story of Ad Spaugh, Cattleman*. New York: Doubleday, Doran and Co., 1940.

Johnson County War. *The Cattle Barons' Rebellion Against Law and Order*. Evanston, Illinois: The Branding Iron Press, 1955. This is the reprint edition of 1,000 copies from the original printing of 1892.

KRAKEL, DEAN F. *The Saga of Tom Horn*. Laramie: Powder River Publishers, 1954. The original version of this book suppressed due to a threatened lawsuit. It gives a valuable insight into the last days of the open range era in Wyoming.

LaFrentz, Ferdinand William. *Cowboy Stuff*. New York: G. P. Putnam's Sons, 1927. This item is of very little historical significance, but it is a beautifully printed, limited edition, written by the longtime secretary of the Swan Land and Cattle Company of Wyoming.

Latham, Dr. Hiram. *Trans-Missouri Stock Raising*. Denver: Old West Publishing Co., 1962. The reprint of the exceedingly rare 1871 edition published in Omaha, Nebraska.

Mercer, Asa Shinn. *The Banditti of The Plains; or, The Cattlemen's Invasion of Wyoming in 1892*. Cheyenne: no publisher given, 1894. This is perhaps the rarest and most choice item of Wyoming range cattle historiography. It deals with the rustlers' perspective of the Johnson County War.

Mokler, Alfred James. *History of Natrona County, Wyoming, 1888–1922*. Chicago: R. R. Donnelley and Sons Co., 1923. Any local history of Wyoming is bound to be strong on cattle material. This is perhaps the best in this line.

Mothershead, Harmon Ross. *The Swan Land and Cattle Company, Ltd*. Norman: University of Oklahoma Press, 1971. A complete study of a representative example and the biggest of the foreign-owned Wyoming cattle operations.

Osgood, Ernest Staples. *The Day of the Cattleman*. Minneapolis: University of Minnesota Press, 1929.

Pelzer, Louis. *The Cattlemen's Frontier: A Record of the Trans-Mississippi Cattle Industry From Ox Trains to Pooling Companies, 1850–1890*. Glendale: The Arthur H. Clark Co., 1936.

Ricketts, William Pendleton. *Fifty Years in the Saddle*. Sheridan: Star Publishing Co., 1942.

Rollinson, John K. *History of the Migration of Oregon-Raised Herds to Mid-Western Markets; Wyoming Cattle Trails*. Caldwell, Idaho: The Caxton Printers, 1948. The first printing of this item was a signed and numbered edition of 1,000 copies.

Rollinson, John K. *Hoofprints of a Cowboy and U.S. Ranger; Pony Trails in Wyoming*. Caldwell, Idaho: The Caxton Printers, 1941.

Shaw, James C. *North From Texas*. Evanston, Illinois: The Branding Iron Press, 1952. This is a reprint edition of 750 copies of the exceedingly rare 1931 first edition.

SHEPHERD, MAJOR WILLIAM. *Prairie Experiences in Handling Cattle and Sheep.* London: Chapman and Hall, Ltd., 1884.

SMITH, HELENA HUNTINGTON. *The War on Powder River.* New York: McGraw-Hill Book Co., 1966. A comprehensive treatment of the Johnson County War.

SPRING, AGNES WRIGHT. *The Cheyenne Club.* Kansas City: Don Ornduff, 1961. A pamphlet issued in a very small edition which gives much of the flavor and style of the eastern and "old country" cattlemen on the Wyoming range in the 1880s.

———. *Seventy Years, a Panoramic History of the Wyoming Stock Growers Association.* Cheyenne: Wyoming Stock Growers' Association, 1942. This is the third authorized historical study of the W.S.G.A.

TRENHOLM, VIRGINIA COLE. *Footprints on the Frontier.* Douglas, Wyoming: Douglas Enterprise Co., 1945. Published in an edition of 1,000 copies.

WEIS, G. *Stock Raising in The Northwest, 1884.* Evanston, Illinois: The Branding Iron Press, 1951.

WISTER, OWEN. *The Virginian: A Horseman of The Plains.* New York: The Macmillan Co., 1902. A classic of American literature, set on the Laramie Plains of Wyoming, included here because of its singular impact on subsequent western fiction.

Wyoming. *Letters From Old Friends and Members of The Wyoming Stockgrowers' Association.* Cheyenne: Wyoming Stock Growers' Association, 1923. This was the first of six historical works published by the W.S.G.A. It is a gem.

Wyoming. *Progressive Men of the State of Wyoming.* Chicago: A. W. Bowen and Company, 1903.